TINSEL TRADING COMPANY

Beautiful Bedrooms
with Ribbons & Trims

The store
across the street...
64 West 38th Street
New York, NY 10018
(212) 354 1242
fax: (212) 354 1319

TiNSEL TRADiNG COMPANY

Beautiful Bedrooms
with Ribbons & Trims

Marcia Ceppos

Foreword by Martha Stewart
Design & Styling by Rosemary Warren
Photography by Art Gray

Sterling Publishing Co., Inc. New York
A Sterling/Chapelle Book

Chapelle, Ltd.

If you have any questions or comments, please contact:
Chapelle, Ltd.
P.O. Box 9252, Ogden, UT 84409
(801) 621-2777 • (801) 621-2788 Fax
e-mail: chapelle@chapelleltd.com
Web site: www.chapelleltd.com

A Red Lips 4 Courage Book
Red Lips 4 Courage Communications, Inc.
8502 E. Chapman Ave., 303
Orange, CA 92869
Web site: www.redlips4courage.com

Library of Congress Cataloging-in-Publication Data

Ceppos, Marcia.
  Tinsel trading company beautiful bedrooms with ribbons & trims / Marcia Ceppos.
     p. cm.
  "A Sterling/Chapelle Book."
  Includes index.
  ISBN 1-4027-2566-3
1. Textile crafts. 2. Interior decoration. 3. House furnishings. I. Title.

TT699.C44 2006
746'.04--dc22

2005023744

10 9 8 7 6 5 4 3 2 1
Published by Sterling Publishing Co., Inc.
387 Park Ave. South, New York, NY 10016
©2006 by Marcia Ceppos
Distributed in Canada by Sterling Publishing
c/o Canadian Manda Group, 165 Dufferin St.
Toronto, Ontario, Canada M6K 3H6
Distributed in the United Kingdom by GMC Distribution Services,
Castle Place, 166 High Street, Lewes, East Sussex, England BN7 1XU
Distributed in Australia by Capricorn Link (Australia) Pty. Ltd.
P.O. Box 704, Windsor, NSW 2756, Australia
Printed and Bound in China
All Rights Reserved
Sterling ISBN-13: 978-1-4027-2566-1
        ISBN-10: 1-4027-2566-3

For information about custom editions, special sales, or premium and corporate purchases, please contact the Sterling Special Sales Department at (800) 805-5489; or e-mail specialsales@sterlingpub.com.

FOREWORD

Endless Treasures at Tinsel Trading Company

My lampshades would be dull, my throw pillows mundane, my tablecloths ordinary, my card table downright unacceptable without the extraordinary adornments that I have discovered over the years at one of my favorite stores in all of the world—Tinsel Trading Co.

I have visited the New York City store, in its original incarnation and in its newly gussied-up state, for many years. I am there several times a year, always searching for the correct length of 2"-wide bronze gold tassel trim for an Italian settee, passementerie for a Chinese lampshade, or just simple sterling silver fabric for a table overlay. Oddly enough, I have always found what I was looking for at Tinsel Trading.

Marcia Ceppos's lovely book *Tinsel Trading Company: Beautiful Bedrooms with Ribbons & Trims* introduces all of us to even more opportunities and possibilities found at this extraordinary establishment.

Martha Stewart

Tinsel Trading Co. has come a long, impressive way from its humble 20th-century beginnings.

"Happiness lies in the joy of achievement and the thrill of creative effort."
—FRANKLIN D. ROOSEVELT

Table of Contents

INTRODUCTION
Once Upon a Time, The Tinsel Trading Story

A long time ago, on the small island known as Manhattan, there was a man who was attracted to shiny and bright gold and silver threads. He grew up to own the most extraordinary inventory from all over the world, having never traveled outside the United States. Following is the story of my grandfather and how Tinsel Trading Company evolved.

After a brief job as a jeep mechanic for the Army during World War I, my grandfather went to work at The French Tinsel Company in Manhattan, the main product being metal threads in an array of styles, colors, and sizes, also known as "tinsel" and made in France. His father was a tailor, so it's not surprising he gravitated toward threads. Metal thread, however, was an unusual choice for an ambitious young man beginning his career. Four years passed and in 1933 my grandfather, Arch J. Bergoffen, purchased the company,

(Above) Arch J. Bergoffen, my grandfather and founder of Tinsel Trading Company.

changed the name, and thus began Tinsel Trading Company.

During World War II, my grandfather's biggest client was the U.S. government. Unable to import metal threads for uniforms, the government relied on my grandfather, who had been warehousing thousands and thousands of spools for years. To this day there remains a large amount of his original inventory in the basement, all on the manufacturers' original wooden spools, paper wrapped with gold labels. Many of them are still in the wooden crates they arrived in from France, never having been opened in more than 70 years.

In the 1950s business took a turn downward. Synthetic threads were being developed monthly, but it was one in particular, Lurex, that ended most of the metal thread business for Tinsel Trading. Lurex is a polyester, metallized thread that is much less expensive, doesn't oxidize, is very strong, and was being manufactured in New York, which made it available to everyone. Technology entered my grandfather's world and the gold rush had ended.

In order to stay in business, it was necessary to expand and offer a wider variety of embellishments. My grandfather, or Mr. B, as he was known, would stay in metals, but now it would include trims, tassels, fringes, cords,

fabrics, and wonders in between. As long as it was made of real metal threads, whether gold, silver, or a rainbow of colors, he would collect and sell it.

Introducing these items allowed Tinsel Trading to expand into new industries. My grandfather supplied twisted metal cords and narrow metal ribbons to the perfume industry. He sold thousands of yards to Chanel and other companies who then tied pieces around the neck of perfume bottles or used it for packaging, giving it a rich, finished look. Another industry he enjoyed success in was the shoe industry. Designers would purchase beautiful metal brocade fabrics for handmade couture shoes.

I remember going to my grandparents' apartment when I was very young and being mesmerized by all the wonderful shiny samples my grandfather had brought home from work. Perhaps it had been predestined, but by the age of 8, I knew what I would do when I grew up. There was no fighting it—it was in my blood.

When I was 11 years old, I started my career "working" at the brand new location of Tinsel Trading Co. Previously it had been wholesale only, in a fourth-floor loft on 36th Street. But in 1969, my grandfather moved to a storefront, where he would begin selling retail as well. The address was 47 West 38th St., where the business has been ever since.

I would travel by subway with my older brother from Queens to Manhattan to help out. Throughout high school and college I worked almost every Saturday and at every other opportunity I could, learning as much as possible about the business.

As I soon realized, it was a family rite of passage to work for Tinsel Trading. My father worked for my grandfather, his new father-in-law, for several years. As a young adult and when the kids were in school, my mother worked for her father too. In their teen years, my two brothers went to work alongside "Poppa." Fast forward to the present, and my two nephews can also list Tinsel Trading on their resumes. Four generations of my family have participated in the evolution of Tinsel Trading.

My Turn

When I graduated high school my intention was to start working full time in the store and skip college. After all, who needed calculus to sell tassels? My family, however, talked me into going to college. I later learned that Tinsel Trading was considered my grandfather's company, and my family assumed that it would fade away over time. They thought by going to college I would choose another career. How wrong they were!

Opening a retail shop was an education for Mr. B. He found out that not everyone was interested in metal trims. He needed more than just his collection of amazing 1920s metal threads, tassels, appliqués, fringes, and fabrics to support his new retail business. He began to accrue everything he could find, from soup to nuts, made before 1960. Somehow word got out, and he never had to travel further than the front door. Everyone who had old stuff lying around, much of it from outside the United States, had heard about this "crazy" guy on 38th Street who would buy almost anything as long as it was old. Little did they know that their supposed "junk" was "gold" to my grandfather.

He bought ribbons, buttons, beads, tassels, and fringes in all colors and fibers— cotton, rayon, silk, and glass. He purchased a large collection of 1950s raffia ornaments made in Italy, dug out Brazilian beetles from the 1930s that had been used in fashions and jewelry, and acquired anything else that attracted him. If it remotely fit into his idea of a creative decorative embellishment, he wanted it.

Hundreds of boxes arrived, many unopened, month after month, year after year. One piece of each item would be put on a shelf to sell, but the rest went into the basement, often piled one box on top of another, blocking aisles and passageways, and mostly sitting unopened and unmarked for years and years. As some of you

(Top and above) These early 1930s French fabrics made from real metal threads are from my grandfather's original inventory. Impossible to reproduce, they are considered museum worthy.

(Above left) That's my grandfather and me in 1979.

(Top) An entire wall in The Store Next Door is dedicated to showcasing the countless choices of vintage and reproduction faux flowers and leaves.

(Above) Wonderful sachets, vintage bridal linens, and other amenities fill this vintage apothecary cabinet.

know, my grandfather was a pack rat and thank goodness he was.

I remember one man he frequently bought from would come to the store with small blue square boxes. As a monthly ritual, he drove up in a station wagon and my grandfather would buy as many as 50 boxes at a time. They would be strategically placed on the floor in the path of customers. In a matter of minutes someone would bump into them, at which my grandfather would proclaim, "You found our special boxes." They would forever be known as the blue box specials.

Years after my grandfather died, I helped empty someone's house of its contents. I parked in the driveway and as I got out of the car I was amazed. There were blue boxes everywhere! I had found the source. There were hundreds and hundreds of boxes in the driveway as well as in the house. Naturally I had to take them. To this day there is still a small section in Tinsel Trading filled with blue boxes, a homage to the past.

Eventually the years of stockpiling turned into decades, and when my grandfather died in 1989 it became my job to try and make sense of thousands and thousands of items and organize it all. I was sure it would only be a matter of a few weeks to get the place together. The innocence of youth! Months went by and I was making little headway. I finally realized that this was no easy task I had undertaken. After all, it had taken more than 50 years to amass this collection and chaos;

it would certainly take a lot longer than a few months to undo it. I was totally overwhelmed by all this and it eventually took many, many years, and a parade of employees, to find a way and develop a plan.

A New Era

In 1998, a new and wonderful era for Tinsel Trading began. Computers were introduced in the store (with me kicking and screaming), we started to exhibit at trade shows, Rosemary Warren freelanced for us doing window displays as well as merchandising, and Martha Stewart came calling.

Long a favorite of Martha's, we had been frequently mentioned in her magazine since its inception in 1990. In October 1998, her staff called, asking if it would be okay to have Martha stop by the store and chat with me for her television show. Would it! The end of the sentence barely out of their mouths, I said yes. After I hung up, I remember thinking that surely I was imagining this. There are thousands of retail stores in New York, yet Martha wanted to highlight Tinsel Trading on national TV.

When the segment aired the first week of December, I was stunned by the immediate reaction to the show. The moment it ended, the phone started ringing and never stopped. Normally slow in the mornings, now people appeared at our doorstep as soon as we opened. To this day there are still customers asking if I was the one on Martha's show.

One of the legacies my grandfather had left me was the retail space almost as cluttered and unorganized as the basement. The disorder and design of the store could not accommodate this many customers. It was obvious changes had to be made. So Rosemary Warren and I redesigned it. We did a complete makeover, ripping out all the furniture, fixtures, lighting, and flooring and starting from scratch. We installed new floors, new lights, and custom-made oak fixtures and furniture. We categorized, colorized, and organized. It was no longer my grandfather's dysfunctional store. We were able to double the size of the space, and it was stunning! Happily, we have been able to keep it that way.

I had tasted a sense of accomplishment. It left me inspired and wanting to do more, so to satisfy this new hunger, in 2002 Tinsel Trading expanded to twice its size. Team Ceppos (that's me) and Warren (that's Rosemary), with assistance from my loyal employees, contractors, and anyone else willing to help, gutted what was once a wholesale clothing company that had left mirrors and metal racks everywhere. Knocking down a part of the shared wall, we made an entrance into the adjoining store, dubbing it The Store Next Door.

Deciding to offer more than trims in our new store, we created small, individual departments for children, tabletop, garden, stationery, and books. We also offer a diverse gift selection, searching out handcrafted artistry collections. Rosemary has

designed the store in beautiful vignettes that are always evolving, and ever changing. With our inventory selling quickly, she re-creates and reinvents each department from season to season.

In 2004, getting the itch again, I opened a third store. Team Ceppos/ Warren got to work, and adding Anna Kapera, we set out to continue the Tinsel tradition of awakening the imagination and offering inspiration, this time in a ribbon store. I found a great location right across the street. The name? The Store Across the Street, of course! Selling every kind of ribbon you can imagine, some designed and produced exclusively for us, the store is stocked floor to ceiling. We have rayon grosgrain, soft satin silk, hundreds of different wired ribbons, luscious 5" wired taffeta, intricately designed jacquards, and lots and lots of vintage. Right after we opened, I bought a warehouse full of 1940s and '50s rayon/cotton petersham grosgrain in all sizes and in the most exquisite colors. I seem to be continuing the tradition of my grandfather. The real challenge will be to keep the aisles clean.

(Top) The Store Across the Street houses most of our ribbon inventory. It is well lit and wonderfully organized—a contrast to the early Tinsel Trading store.

(Above) A treasured antique ribbon cabinet holds a place of honor in the store.

(Left) The basement at Tinsel Trading is still filled with years of treasures although it's better organized than when this photo was taken.

(Top and above) Throughout this book you will find inspiring projects made with ribbons, trims, flowers, and countless other embellishments.

A Novel Idea

Sharing the fabulous products we work with in a book was a natural next step. As with all of the things we have done, it was a team effort. We decided to ask some of the wonderful designers who also are our customers to participate in creating a series of bedrooms inspired by the seasons. They eagerly responded by fashioning some of the most beautiful things I have ever seen.

I have been asked, "Why a bedroom book?" Well, it is a place where you spend an enormous amount of time. Okay, so most of it is sleeping. You deserve to have the most beautiful and the most romantic room, even if you are the only one in it. These surroundings are the first you see waking up. How wonderful to choose something that will make you smile.

Everyone can be an artist. Even if it is as simple as gluing a flower or appliqué onto a slipper or adding a tassel to a key, it all becomes artistry. Choosing color, size, style, and placement are all your decisions and therefore you can create something special and unique that becomes art.

While not everything you see in these bedrooms is from my stores, the styles and taste all reflect an image and lifestyle that has been Tinsel Trading for more than 70 years. It has been mentioned many times that I am Tinsel and Tinsel is me, or you can take Marcia out of Tinsel (pushing and shoving), but you can't take Tinsel out of Marcia. With that in mind, my variety of tastes and attitudes are all reflected in my stores and these bedrooms. Rosemary Warren, having known me for more than a decade, is able to interpret my thoughts and ideas and make them reality. Minimal, clean, lush, and enticing —that's how I see these bedrooms.

I have shared Tinsel Trading's history with you and hope you have enjoyed it. If I am able to hold your attention until the end of the book, I am humbled by your interest. I feel proud that I was chosen to carry on the name and reputation started by my grandfather. I know I speak for everyone at Tinsel Trading, The Store Next Door, and The Store Across the Street when I say we are honored and grateful to be able to work with the most fabulous, exquisite trims. We all feel a sense of history and enormous respect for the items we sell. I have a wonderful staff and I hope one day you are able to meet them and allow them to share our world with you. Perhaps you might even become as drawn to these beautiful trims as we are.

I hope we inspire you to create some of the projects presented in this book and that you will visit us at Tinsel Trading soon. And if you're out of town and aren't planning a trip to New York anytime soon, please visit us at www.tinseltrading.com.

Marcia Ceppos

P.S. Stay tuned, I know there is more to come! In fact, I seem to have an itch starting…

CHAPTER 1

The Spring Bedroom

Spring is a wonderful time of year. Living in a cold climate, spring allows us to shake off the snow and cold, put away our heavy coats, and open the windows to watch nature blossom. The buds on the trees start to appear as the ground begins to warm. The flowers stretch out their arms and pop up their heads—ready or not, here I come! It's the season of rebirth, and we look forward to spending time outdoors, where everything seems brighter and more alive. ■

■ Nature in Bloom

What better season than spring for a room that's simple, clean, and humble, decorated in my favorite style—Shaker? The four-poster bed in this room commands attention. Thin, straight lines convey a sense of openness and comfort.

I love the warmth of the wood tones in the bare floor and the sunlight streaming through the sheer curtains. You can keep a room modest and intimate while still embellishing with trims, flowers, and an array of other details.

You can enjoy a room this simple without it becoming too frilly or fussy. We were able to embellish to our heart's content, and it was as simple as using a glue gun.

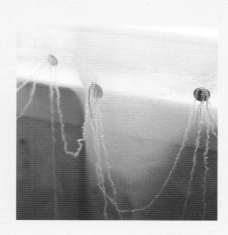

Drapes
with Detail

Waking up in a room filled with pink light is wonderful and romantic. Ethereal, sheer curtains designed by Michael Schultz bring the beauty of natural light into the room. Curtains like these guard privacy while still allowing maximum sunlight in the room. Adding faux flowers along the top of the curtain is a finishing touch that literally blossoms. Rather than heavy tiebacks, Michael threaded iridescent eyelash yarn through vintage metal spangles to create a delicate look.

Embellished Painting

I rescued this painting from a flea market and decided it needed something to spice it up. It felt like I was creating my own masterpiece—move over Pablo! I took great pride and care in selecting the perfect materials, adding paper and fabric flowers to reflect what was already painted on the canvas. It brought the painting to life with a three-dimensional effect, and now, in my opinion, it is a very unique picture. This innovative technique can be used on photos, magazine pages, or any other image you want to embellish. ◄

Beaded Slippers

Everyone owns a pair of slippers, however, few of us have something this lovely in our closet. Leslie Korda may have designed these fabulous slippers imagining them next to a bed in a tropical paradise, with the ocean a few feet away and the breeze blowing through shuttered windows. Snap out of it and come back to reality. We do have a bed and a window, at least. Do a tropical kimono and a green wicker chair count? Since an island is out of the question for most of us, you can still create the environment with custom slippers and a favorite chair. A beaded leaf, a small flower bud, and a little glue, and like magic an ordinary pair of slippers becomes an artful luxury. ►

■ Peeling on Purpose

One look at the walls in my bedroom and some people suggest I should have fired my contractor. After taking down three layers of hideous wallpaper, and knowing there were many more to follow, I took a break and left the room. When I walked back in, the afternoon sun was streaming through the windows. I was speechless as I stood in the doorway because the room had an amazing glow. It may be a bit of an exaggeration to say a choir was singing too, but that is how it hit me. I knew I had to throw away the extra-large razor blade and pail of water and proclaim the job well done and complete. Some visitors look at the walls and ask when they will be finished, while others beg for the tele-phone number of my decorator. I just smile, thankful that I do not need to peel away any more wallpaper.

■ Dressed to Shade

Since this spring bedroom has flowers galore, it's only natural to continue the theme on this lampshade designed by Melissa Neufeld. It is unnecessary to settle for a plain shade when you can transform one into something special. When you open your options of fabrics to anything you can imagine—a dress you've grown out of or even your favorite jeans with all the holes—your design choices are limitless. Once the fabric is on the shade, add ribbons and trims, and voilá!

■ Pretty Portrait

New life was brought to an old frame by covering it with fabric and adding trim, flowers, and appliqués. The beautiful frame called for something special to place in it, so a woman's portrait was chosen.

■ Trimmed Shams

There is something about crisp, white ironed pillow shams—of course, embellished with a few trims—that look fantastic on a bed. Green velvet geranium leaves on the pillow sham reflect the room's garden theme. Simple, clean, and green—perfect for this room.

A watermelon/green contemporary ribbon fed through a vintage piece of lace pulls in color from the rest of the room's décor. With these easy touches an ordinary sham becomes extra special. You can duplicate the look of high-end bedding and have a one-of-a-kind design at the same time.

■ Hat Hang-Ups

A simple straw hat becomes a thing of beauty when it is decorated with millinery flowers and beautiful ribbons. While vintage flowers have a patina and charm, there are also many reproductions available that are just as appealing. We should know—we have shelves full of them!

It has become cliché to hang coats or dining chairs from pegs on the wall. Anyone can do it, and many have. What about something more unusual? Try decorated hats on the pegs. It may have been done before, but perhaps not as beautifully. A well-loved hat adorned with gobs of ribbons and flowers is a very personal accessory. When I look at these hats, my imagination starts drifting and I see myself strolling in a garden.

■ Embellished Vignettes

Vignettes create interest and intrigue. Visually attractive, they become the focus when entering a room. Even on a humble pine dresser, several vignettes tell a story. A collection of wooden boxes containing jewelry and charms, whimsical childhood keepsakes, tiny sterling silver frames, and fairy bottles that hold dreams for safekeeping complete an interesting assemblage of treasures. The small collection of Ms also tells a story.

Mirror Garland

Rosemary Warren made an enchanting garland for the mirror that had belonged to my paternal grandmother, mixing vintage crepe paper with contemporary fabric flowers. A garland also makes a delightful festoon for a mantel, table, or just about any another piece of furniture you'd like to dress up.

While I look forward to springtime, I can hardly wait to get out in the garden and plant. There can never be enough flowers in the world. Of course there can never be enough faux flowers either. Books, boxes, mirrors, and photo albums all should have flowers on them. They brighten up everything!

■ Covered Books

I'm sure by now you know that flowers make me happy. Kaari Meng
seems to feel the same way. Elegant vintage flowers adorn the front of
her photo albums and journals to enhance an otherwise simple book.
Covered with linen, they are truly beautiful. ▲

■ Good Things, Small Boxes

Anna Corba has taken ordinary, everyday boxes and embellished them
with pretty ribbons, flowers, and buttons, creating wonderful containers
for all those bits of paper, receipts, and other odds and ends we are
all likely to misplace. Boxes such as these can be fashioned to suit your
own taste. ◀

Sitting Pretty

In today's society, where it is necessary to multitask and rooms need to be multifunctional, it is a pleasure that some bedrooms are big enough to accommodate sitting rooms, especially ones with lots of windows. Hanging the same pink curtains that Michael Schultz designed for the bedroom makes this a glorious place to read a book or plan your next party, or even help you decide where to use more flowers and ribbons.

Embellished Hat

The garden theme of the springtime room continues with a neatly folded stack of fine linens. Rather than storing them in a drawer or closet, keep linens out to be admired. Top off the display with a garden hat decorated with a fine velvet ribbon and a beautiful silk garden rose.

■ Fairy Bottles

Bottles created by Elaine Seamans contain wonderful sentiments, memories, and wishes. Start with an empty bottle, embellish it with items that reflect your personal style, and keep your most treasured thoughts contained closely at hand. Beautiful ribbon and trim are all it takes to decorate the bottleneck.

Captured Hopes & Dreams

Fallen Faerie Wings

Fallen Stars

Laundry Bag

While it looks too beautiful to easily guess its purpose, this lovely bag
is for laundry. Kaari Meng designed this stunning "sack" made of linen
and vintage flowers and raffia ornaments. It seems far too wonderful for
grimy clothes. Perhaps it should be reserved for hand washables. Hung
on a cabinet door, the laundry bag is convenient for use.

2

The Summer Bedroom

When I think of summer, I smell flowers in bloom and see flut-terbies flitting about. Birds are singing and chirping, and pesky crows are squawking. I taste barbecue hamburgers and hot dogs, and I drool thinking about burning marshmallows for s'mores. I imagine building sand condos at the beach, listening to waves crash in the ocean, or swimming in a pool. I begin to feel sticky from the heat and humidity. I envision pinks, greens, and other bright colors and lots of sunlight. ■

■ Flowers & Butterflies

The summer bedroom brings fond memories and emotions to life. Sunlight streams in to awaken at dawn. At night a gorgeous chandelier made of ribbons, beads, and ornaments lights up the room. Brilliant colors surround the room, and of course, flowers are everywhere. Flowers and butterflies on the pillowcases, flowers in vases on the night-stand, and flowers blooming on the duvet. There are flowers on the clothes hamper, on slip-pers, and even on a handbag.

Posy Pillowcase

Velvet flowers, vintage leaves, and felt appliqués, along with a wonderful tassel, take a pillowcase from functional to fabulous. Fun details on ordinary bed linens customize the look to reflect your personality. ▲

Blooming Bed Linens

Richie Rich and Traver Rains are designers in the fashion industry. They wanted to be a part of the summer bedroom because they had an outrageous idea. Did they ever! They presented me with an explosion of colors on the most extraordinary, fun linens I had ever seen. As you may notice, the duvet is encrusted with flowers, appliqués, fringe, and felt balls in every bright color imaginable. It's the quintessential look of Richie and Traver. ◄

Fluffed-Up Slippers

The summer bed linens inspired me to join in and be a part of the summer bedroom. Normally I am designing trims, never sure where they will end up, so I had fun redirecting my thoughts to a finished product. I rose to the challenge, and decided to transform a pair of everyday slippers. I went to our wall display of flowers and the appliqué section, pulling elements that matched the linens designed by Richie and Traver. What fun I had—my first designer footwear! It's almost impossible to tell where the duvet ends and the slippers begin. ▲

Summer Duvet

Richie and Traver planted a virtual garden in the corner of the summer duvet. Using a rainbow of colors, they combined vibrant flowers with fringe and pompom trim. ◄

Trimmed Linens

Waking up with wonderful visions of butterflies and hearts floating around in your head, summer is the season to jump out of bed, excited for the day to begin. Waking up among these colors brings you to life and gets you ready to go. Say goodbye to perfectly ironed white shams, and hello to exotic dreams on a tropical island with vividly colored parrots flying overhead. Get out your Hawaiian shirt and watch for falling coconuts!

■ Garden Shams

While these pillow shams are best used just for show and not to actually rest upon, they are a delight. The design is all about fun, color, and fantasy. Notice how each tassel is a different color, yet they tie in with the scheme of the flowers and appliqués. Adding the mini pompom fringe along the border of the pillowcase adds playfulness and motion. Think of fields of wildflowers swaying in the wind and everywhere you look you see blossoms, leaves, and butterflies.

Laundry Hamper

I love this vintage white wicker hamper that was purchased at a flea
market. It's a classic beauty. Because it is all white, it desperately
needed some pizzazz. It absolutely screamed for flowers. What
a surprise—I happen to have loads of them! Inspired to design,
I stepped in. The hamper was going into the summer bedroom
so I decided to keep it simple. I added flowers to the corners and
tassels to the handles and at the top for easy opening. It is colorful
and simple—mission accomplished.

■ Cascading Flower Pillow

Switching pillows can change the look of a bed, which can be refreshing. Add cascading flowers to a pillowcase and voilá—instant change. Bouquets of flowers are attached to the top and a few blossoms are placed randomly on the body of the pillow for a casual, scattered effect. Simply gather the flowers into bunches, bind the stems together by wrapping them with thread, and sew them to the pillow. Large, white pillow shams behind the floral masterpiece provide the perfect subdued background.

Musical Memo Board

The fun, decorative bulletin board hanging behind the flowers was designed by Anna Corba. Gone are the days of using plain cork boards to hang your important notes. Anna has used sheet music as the background for her board, however, any favorite paper will work. Simply add a few ornaments, buttons, flowers, and a wonderful ribbon to hang the bulletin board. ▲

Forever Flowers

Sitting on the table by the window, my collection of vintage matte white vases are filled with flowers. Yes, you guessed it—faux flowers. The arrangement includes long-stemmed bright orange poppies, yellow parrot tulips, purple pansies, and pink and magenta violets. Set against a white tablecloth in white vases, these vivid summer colors seemingly jump out at you. All that's missing is the mint julep! ◄

Ribbon Clutch

A delightful clutch is the perfect accessory for a summer girl's night out. Lorren Bell designed this hot pink diva handbag. It is completely covered with glamorous ribbon and accented with a large, fluffy handmade silk flower. Design your own handbag with the miles and miles of ribbon and flowers found at Tinsel Trading. The exciting part about this project is the endless possibilities to make a handbag to match any outfit, in any color or style you like. Eat your heart out, Coach!

Jewel of Light

When I first saw this chandelier, I was speechless. I had seen the ugly duckling before it was transformed by Gerard Yosca, acclaimed jewelry designer and Tinsel Trading's neighbor in New York City. Its finished beauty is almost too fantastic to believe. Colorful glass beads, fabulous ribbon, decorative ornaments, and wire were used to convert a common, ordinary light into a Venetian-style fixture. Hanging a chandelier in the bedroom might seem extravagant to some, but for me it provides an elegance and glamour that is well deserved.

3

The Autumn Bedroom

Autumn is a time of transition. Leaves are turning wondrous colors, flowers are starting to fade as they prepare their roots for the coming season, and we cherish the last of the warm days. I spend extra time making sure the arrival of autumn in my home is a welcome and comforting season. Colors are integral to this feeling. Earth tones in shades of brown and gold help lead us into the chill of autumn well prepared. ■

Season of Comfort

This bedroom is a wonderful mix of styles. It combines American Indian influence with a Spanish/Mexican feeling, adding in a little western style. The magnificent rope bed is from the 1880s, and throughout the rest of the room are antique accents that further add to a primitive feel that evokes a sense of history. This room proves that ribbons and trims aren't just confined to feminine and romantic styles. Everything about this room creates an environment that is comforting and soothing.

Trimmed Linens

Guillermo Guerra created a sense of style simply with the use of ribbons. Using brown and white ribbon to trim pillowcases in a vertical stripe transformed basic cream-colored linens into a rich element of luxury.

■ Western Walls

Walls can play a significant part in the ambiance of a room. The wall treatment in the autumn room suggests age and mirrors the theme of the décor. It is the result of stripping old flocked wallpaper and leaving the underbelly of paper exposed, casting a suede-like appearance on the walls. Incorporate leather lacing on a parchment lampshade and it instantly becomes a western-style shade that's a darn good match for the room. ▲

■ Fringe-Top Drapes

This vignette displays a wonderful marriage of wicker and rattan. Highlighting the blanket collection is a vintage American Indian wedding blanket. Fringe down the running edge of the drape adds style and texture. ►

■ Suitcase Accents

A wonderful collection of stacked vintage suitcases can be placed
strategically to mask a multitude of unwanted sights. These hide
a wall-mounted air conditioner. They also double as storage space.
Adding tassels to complement the colors in the room ties the whole
look together.

Easy, Elegant Valance

Beautiful linen drapes are complemented by this stunning imported acorn fringe and superb trim simply sewn to the top. If you look carefully at the insert panel in the duvet on pages 58-59, you will see that the drape and bed fabrics coordinate well and are a perfect fit. ◄

Creative Tieback

To create a more elegant window treatment, a cranberry-colored vintage silk fabric was made into a bustle and tied back onto the wall. These spectacular handcrafted gold metal tassels hanging from a grosgrain ribbon bow exquisitely complement the fabrics. ►

Embellished Workspace

Among the items in my home workspace is my grandfather's jewelry chest from the 1890s. This was the first thing I saw whenever I went into my grandparents' apartment.

Placing treasured items in a prominent place keeps memories close to your heart. I am reminded of my grandfather every day at work, but at home this box enables me to value personal memories of him.

There are no limits to the imagination, as evidenced by the embellished box next to the lamp. Using an assortment of components such as silver metal trim, tassels, fringe, and wooden spools, this container can hold jewelry, pocket change, or cherished love letters. The continuity of color brings together this eclectic collection of desktop amenities.

▪ Leaf Wreath Picture

Melissa Neufeld has created a wreath of leaves framing a montage of textiles, paper, and graphics. Using fabric flowers to showcase a composition fashions a timeless classic.

Setting up a vignette of favorite items clearly expresses individuality. This collection of initials personalizes a private space. Other carefully chosen objects work together to set a mood and convey a sense of style.

■ Hand-Decorated Books

Books that have been decorated add a personal, artistic touch to encasing your private notes. Nancy Rosin chose this project since vintage paper is near and dear to her heart. With the use of trims and fringe, you can conceal the ordinary and beautifully enhance a portfolio. Once you decorate your first book, you will want to start a whole library.

Recycled Bottles

Clear glass bottles are fascinating to me—the way the light reflects and distorts the surroundings when you look through them. Elaine Seamans has many fun and fantastic ideas for recycling empty bottles. She suggests saving mementos and photographs inside, or using an inspirational statement as a label. ▲

Head Dressed

Atop the 1930s California Monterey dresser stands a vintage jewelry display head. She is modeling a handmade headdress fashioned from vintage flowers and leaves. Perfume bottles, feathers, and an antique vanity set echo the primitive atmosphere of the room. ◄

■ Mixing Colors

Autumn is such an inspiring season that we designed more than one room to accommodate our ideas. This bedroom is absolutely stunning. The saffron glow engulfs you the moment you open your eyes in the morning. When I stand in this room, I feel safe and calm, yet full of energy. I love mixing different woods because it brings out the warmth in the room. All of the colors—from the silk curtains to the blankets, lampshade, and flowers—coordinate and match beautifully. Looking at this room brings to mind fallen autumn leaves.

A once-bright wallpaper was dramatically changed to alter the tone of the room. A sienna tint mixed with a wall glaze was applied to the existing wallpaper. The smoky richness of the walls now adds another layer and dimension to the room.

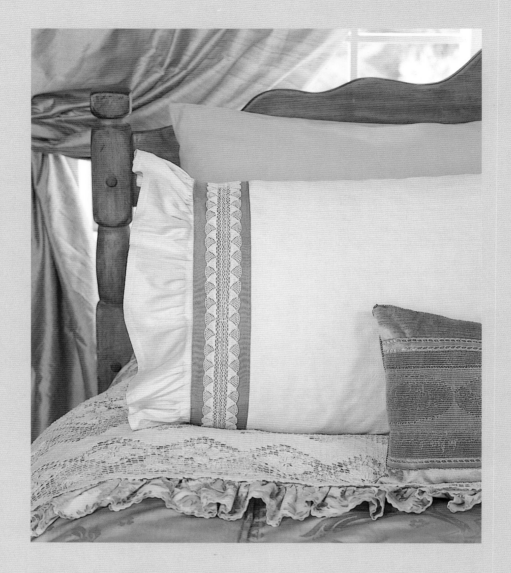

Dupioni Pillowcases

Guillermo Guerra designed these charming ruffled ivory dupioni silk pillowcases. Because there are so many patterns in the room, keeping them simple is a nice touch. Guillermo enhanced the romance of the bedroom by adding lace on top of amber-colored ribbon. Simply by changing the color of the ribbon you can have several beautiful sets of pillowcases.

Drapery Trim

Adding a fancy decorative trim to the top of these dupioni silk drapes gives them texture. Choosing a solid color for the drapes helps achieve a lightness to complement the dark, rich furniture. At sunset this room is ablaze with color. The reflection of the drapery illuminates pumpkin tones across the walls and bed. ▲

Fancy Tiebacks

These tiebacks are extraordinary and are unlike any I have ever seen before. The tassels are flat rather than round, the ties are made of a woven trim rather than cording, and the rosettes, which act as appliqués, are wonderful. ◄

■ Old Masters Florals

The florals arranged in Dutch style on the bureau are wonderfully realistic. They pick up the accent colors of the room perfectly. It's amazing what carefully selected faux flowers can do for a room. If you look closely, you can see insects nibbling away and bees pollinating the flowers.

Adding personal touches like pictures and sachets enrich a room. These small details are an easy way to change and refresh your space, and can reflect your mood at the time. They also can bring comfort and joy when needed most.

◼ Pillow Sachets

To bring color continuity to the room, Rosemary Warren designed these sachets in teal using vintage brocade fabric. Tie a grosgrain or velvet ribbon around each sachet and arrange them in threes or fours for an interesting display. ▲

◼ Luxurious Lampshade

The floral theme throughout the bedroom continues with the lamp-shade on an alabaster base. The focal point of the shade is a magnificent 1890s French silk chenille appliqué that reflects the rich colors of the room. Personal touches make a bedroom comfortable and inviting. ◀

◼ Embellished Hutch

What was once a china hutch now proudly houses sweaters, scarves,
and hats. The weathered turquoise patina of the paint pulls the room
together. Glass beaded trim is used to decorate the shelves, while a pair
of beautiful tassels dresses up the piece for its new use. Trims can be
easily added to shelves for a more finished look.

4

The Winter Bedroom

Winter is my favorite season. I was born in the middle of a blizzard, and have always thought there was a connection. Living in New York my entire life has also made winter a very special season to me. In anticipation of the holidays, bright lights and tourists are everywhere. Store windows are dressed to the nines with sounds of holiday music coming from outdoor speakers. Nature, however, plans for the opposite. The ground is brown and frozen, the landscape dreary, and plants and trees are seemingly lifeless. ■

■ A Time to Hibernate

No wonder animals take this time to hole up out of sight. With temperatures dropping and snow falling, it's the ideal time to curl up in front of the fireplace and hibernate.

The décor of a nurturing winter bedroom feeds into our instinct to hide away. The fire sets the mood, the rich, dark colors create a sense of warmth, and the deep wood tones of the bed and mantel all create a feeling of contentment. There are enough logs for a fire, and the breakfast tray on the bed reminds me that the kitchen is nearby and functioning. Once snuggled in, I could stay for the duration.

■ Layering Pillows

Pillows, pillows, and more pillows—you can never have enough pillows!
There are no rules about how many pillows are allowed on a bed, so use
as many as you like. When displaying them, keep in mind that varieties
in pattern and texture always add depth to the visual presentation.

Ribbon Bolster

Linda Ashton designed a magnificent bolster. Except for the base fabric and the rosette tassel, every inch of it is made from ribbon. The eye cannot help but be drawn to the different textures and patterns. ▲

Lavender-Filled Pillow

Kaari Meng designed this lavender-filled pillow around the vintage floral brocade centerpiece fabric. A handsome gold metal trim bordering the center highlights the fabric and adds to the striking look of the pillow. ▲

■ Bed Tray

A fire roaring away, candles lit, lavender-filled pillows, and now breakfast in bed. It doesn't get much better than this! Jill Schwartz created
this fantastic bed tray, which in its former life had been a drawer.
Ribbons, flowers, paint, and other assorted goodies are all that's
needed to rejuvenate an old and unused piece of wood that was likely
destined for the trash.

Decoupage Lampshade

Decoupage is a wonderful art that allows you to adhere any paper material to a flat surface to create an entirely new look. Take a favorite photo, a page from a book, or a special drawing from your child and turn it into a functional piece of art. Kaari Meng, using decoupage and images of green birds in flight, created this charming feathery green lampshade. ◄

Vanity Trinket Box
& Powder Puff Wand

Silk ribbon roses on vanity accessories dates back to Victorian times. Considered an Old World technique, Carole Sidlow has been hand making these since she was a teen. Sitting on the tray is a hand-held mirror and a round box adorned with a luscious silk rose. A plain perfume bottle also can be transformed simply by hanging a metal tassel around the neck. ►

■ Mantel Magic

A mantel beautifully decorated with a wreath and garland brings nature and the great smell of pine into the room. Keeping the cuttings simple and undecorated allows you to enjoy the freshness throughout the season without screaming holiday. We arranged vintage vases filled with a bounty of faux flowers on the mantel. Roses, tulips, and pansies abound even though they are well out of season.

Trimmed Chair

An upholstered chair can become a showpiece by adding magnificent tassel trim. The trim shows exceptionally well on this chair because the raised legs allow the tassels to hang freely to the floor and are not obstructed by a fabric skirt. ◄

Silver Tieback

The main attraction to this glorious window treatment is a spectacular 19th-century silver metal double tassel tieback. While this handsome tieback was certainly meant for a mansion, it would be just as magnificent in a cottage. ►

Velvet Drapes

This warm winter sitting area is the ultimate in comfort. Lush velvet drapes help keep out winter drafts. Edging the drapes with a contrasting color of cream lace is a simple and wonderful accent that makes the room rich and elegant. ◄

Room to Daydream

This dayroom allows light to flood in and is a welcome escape from the weariness of the season. Decorated in winter white, the room invites all of the accessories to stand out so that the details can be appreciated.

■ Crocheted Pillow

This extraordinary pillow is from Tinsel Trading's exclusive collection of crocheted pillows. They are handmade by an associate's mother in Poland. I send vintage metal threads to her and she sends me back intricate, remarkable designs either as pillows or doilies in an assortment of sizes and shapes. Placing this one pillow on the chaise showcases it as a work of art.

■ Ribbon Frame

A ribbon-covered photo frame is easy to make and becomes the focal
point of a tableside vignette. Mixing fresh and faux flowers is a lovely way
to incorporate out-of-season flowers into a setting.

Parasol Lampshade

Decorating this fantastic paper parasol was the idea of Jill Schwartz. Embellish a parasol or umbrella with flowers, fringe, and appliqués. We imagined it as a lampshade and attached it to a wrought-iron torchere found at a flea market. To complete the design, use a tassel for the pull chain. ◄

Bulletin Dress Form

Rosemary Warren transformed an old dress form into a bulletin board. Costumed with a white lace tablecloth and cherry velvet ribbon around the body, this beauty is an incredible concept. Attached with personal mementos, photographs, and tokens of love, the dress form is used as inspiration to empower her creative energy. ►

95

Winter Loft Bedroom

Our second winter bedroom, in the spirit of an open loft space, is a delightful contrast to a darker style. Minimal in elements and inspired by Shaker design, it evokes feelings of serenity and provides a refreshing sanctuary. It is the perfect décor for introspection and reflection. Almost monastic, the room is uncluttered, yet we found embellishing with trims very easy.

Uncomplicated Style

A Windsor bench set in front of bright windows makes a simple spot to rest or read. The details of the wreath and footstool are enough to carry the setting, proving that embellishing a room doesn't have to be complicated or too detailed. ▲

Tudor Footstool

Melissa Neufeld reworked and redesigned this flea-market find, creating something elegant. The footstool was given a complete makeover using paint, ribbon, and metal trim to achieve a Tudor look. ►

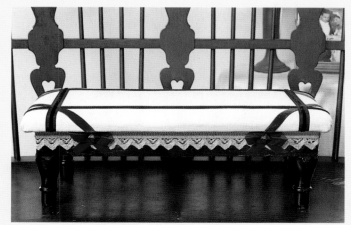

Tablecloth Curtain

Light filters through a crochet tablecloth used as a curtain, creating shadow patterns across the pillow tops. Swags of 1900s French silver trim adorn the curtain. On each corner hangs a beaded gold glass tassel. ◄

Metal Fabric Runner

French fabric from the 1920s made from metal threads can be used as a shawl or table runner, or simply draped over a chair. This fabric is decorated with vintage military trim, modern gold lace, and a vintage silver tassel. ►

■ Winter Wreath

A wreath, which hangs over the bench, warms the room with romantic
reds mixing new and vintage millinery flowers that are lightly sprinkled
with glass glitter. By setting the wreath apart from the other elements
in the room, its uniqueness is highlighted.

Project Instructions

Drapes With Detail

By Michael Schultz

Page 18

MATERIALS

- Faux flowers: 11 bunches, vintage, mixed colors and varieties
- Needle
- Silk organza: cream, 2 1/2 yards; rose, 2 1/2 yards
- Silver spangles/piattes: 9
- Thread: cream
- Tinsel: 10 yards, vintage

TOOLS

- Scissors
- Straight pins

INSTRUCTIONS

Step 1: Snip fabric 1/2" on selvage and tear entire length of both fabrics.

Step 2: Measure cream organza to dimensions of window, and tear them to size. Window shown is 78". Tearing fabric gives it an ethereal feel.

Step 3: Measure rose fabric to 78", snip 1/2" in and tear.

Step 4: Measure rose fabric to 40", snip 1/2" in and tear to size. This will give you two pieces of rose fabric.

Step 5: Cut one 2 1/2"-wide strip of cream fabric. Cut this strip into five 6" strips. These will be used for curtain loops.

Step 6: Pull all stray threads from fabric.

Step 7: Take two pieces of rose fabric and overlay and attach them together with all nine silver spangles equally placed along folded edge.

Step 8: Sew on curtain loops. Attach faux flowers where desired.

Embellished Painting

By Marcia Ceppos

Page 19

MATERIALS

- Faux flowers: assorted
- Faux stamens and leaves: assorted
- Painting or photo

TOOLS

- Hot glue gun

INSTRUCTIONS

Step 1: Choose your artwork. *Note:* Use a painting or photo with no intrinsic value, or a photocopy of one. Uncle Sammy's paint-by-number is okay, and so is Aunt Bertha's clown on black velvet.

Step 2: Beginning with leaves, glue to picture, adding individual petals or single stems as desired. Add as many elements as you'd like. Try to complement, rather than cover up, artist's original intention.

Beaded Slippers

By Leslie Korda
Page 19

MATERIALS

■ Beaded leaves: 2

■ Faux flowers: 2

■ Narrow ribbon: burgundy, 1 yard

■ Slippers: straw, raffia, or other fairly smooth material

TOOLS

■ Hot glue gun or fabric glue

■ Scissors

INSTRUCTIONS

Step 1: Measure length of inside of inner sole and cut narrow ribbon to fit.

Step 2: Glue narrow ribbon about 1/2" from outside edge of inner sole.

Step 3: Shape beaded leaves so they fit curve of top of slipper; glue one beaded leaf to top of each slipper. Apply glue along entire underside edge of leaf and along spine. Press and hold in place until dry.

Step 4: Glue faux flower to top outer side of slipper.

Step 5: Repeat with other slipper.

Dressed to Shade

By Melissa Neufeld
Page 22

MATERIALS

■ Fabric: 1/2 yard for bias trim (solid shown in project)

■ Fabric: 1 yard for shade (floral print shown in project)

■ Lampshade

■ Pencil

■ Ribbon: 1/2" wide, long enough to crisscross width of shade twice

■ Ribbon: 1" wide, length of top circumference of shade

■ Ribbon: 1 1/2" wide, 2 1/2 times

longer than bottom circumference of shade (1 1/2" and 2" ribbons should be contrasting colors)

- Ribbon: 2" wide, 2 1/2 times longer than bottom circumference of shade

- Spray glue

- Tracing paper

TOOLS

- Hot glue gun or fabric glue

- Scissors

- Sewing machine

INSTRUCTIONS

Step 1: Using piece of tracing paper large enough to cover half of lampshade, place paper over shade and trace top, bottom, and sides. Cut out shape and use it as pattern to cut two pieces of fabric. Lay both pieces of fabric over shade to make sure it fits properly. If it is larger than shade, trim it.

Step 2: Spray backside of one piece of fabric with spray glue and adhere to shade. Smooth out wrinkles and bubbles as you go. Repeat for second piece of fabric.

Step 3: Cut 1 1/2" strip of fabric

on bias, long enough to cover two overlapping edges of fabric on shade. Iron into bias tape, and using hot glue gun or fabric glue, adhere on overlapping edges of fabric on sides of shade.

Step 4: Take narrow coordinating ribbon and, attaching it at top and bottom of shade, crisscross entire shade at width.

Step 5: Take two ribbons for bottom of shade and lay 1 1/2" ribbon over 2" ribbon. Sew gathering stitch down center of ribbons. *Note:* Another option is to lay string down center of ribbons and run zigzag stitch down length of string.

Step 6: Gather running stitch or string to ruffle length of bottom of shade. Attach to bottom of shade with glue, overlapping just a little at end.

Step 7: To finish shade, glue ribbon around top edge of shade.

Mirror Garland

By Rosemary Warren
Page 29

MATERIALS

- Blossom branches: 6

- Floral tape: moss green

- Floral wire: green

- Gardenia: large, 1

- Gardenias: small, 5

- Leaves: cut from vintage green crepe paper

- Pink roses: 12

INSTRUCTIONS

Note: Flowers and branches are faux flowers; leaves are made with vintage crepe paper. You may substitute silk leaves.

Step 1: Cut floral wire desired length of garland plus 4". Make 2" loop and twist at end to create hook. Repeat for other end of wire.

Step 2: Using 12" of floral tape at a time, lay one flower and 3-4 leaves on wire. Wrap tape around each flower and leaf. Stretch tape as you wrap so it sticks in place. Adhere large gardenia at center.

Continue layering and wrapping until you come to 3" before end of wire.

Step 3: When you reach end of wire, place last group of blossom and leaves facing opposite direction. Wrap firmly in place. Garland can be hung from small nails; loops serve as hooks.

Covered Books

By Kaari Meng

Page 31

MATERIALS

- Blank book: journal, guestbook, or scrapbook

- Buttons and beads

- Fabric: white or cream linen, enough to cover book

- Millinery leaves, flowers, and stamen

- Ribbon

- Straight pins

TOOLS

- Hot glue gun or fabric glue

- Scissors

- Sewing machine

INSTRUCTIONS

Step 1: Wrap and fit fabric to book. Use straight pins to be sure fit is right. Remove and cut fabric to size of book.

Step 2: Using sewing machine, stitch book cover and place on book.

Step 3: Decorate with millinery flowers, ribbon, and notions by using hot glue gun or fabric glue. While making these books, imagine old corsages worn to school dances in the 1930s.

Good Things, Small Boxes

By Anna Corba

Page 31

Large Box

MATERIALS

- Craft glue

- Double-stick tape

- Fabric daisies: 4

- Kraft box: vanilla or white, 9" x 7" x 6"

- Printed note card

- Ribbon: 1/2" sage grosgrain, 5 yards; 1" pink polka dot grosgrain, 1 yard; 1" striped grosgrain, 2 yards; 1 1/2" sage grosgrain, 2 yards

- Rubber stamps

- Spray mount adhesive

TOOLS

- Decorative edge scissors

- Scissors

- Sewing scissors

INSTRUCTIONS

Step 1: Cut 1 1/2" sage grosgrain and 1" striped grosgrain into two lengths, one at 21" and the other at 23". This will give you four pieces of ribbon.

Step 2: Place 1" pieces of double-stick tape at 1" intervals on one side of all ribbon pieces.

Step 3: Remove box lid. Working with box bottom: At 9" side, beginning with 21" piece of wide grosgrain, wrap 1" over top edge of box at center and stick to inside of box. Wrap ribbon underneath box and up back side, flapping remaining 1" over top of box. Press firmly to secure tape.

Step 4: Repeat over sage ribbon with 21" length of striped ribbon.

Step 5: Turning box to 7" side, repeat steps 3 and 4 with 23" ribbon lengths.

Step 6: Cut 1/2" sage ribbon into four pieces of 21" length and four pieces of 23" length. Measure in 1" from all box corners and attach 1/2" sage ribbon in same manner.

Step 7: Working with box lid: Cut pink polka dot grosgrain to 32". Tape 1" pieces of double-stick tape at 1" intervals to one side of ribbon. Beginning at back of box, press ribbon firmly into place around side of lid.

Step 8: Using decorative edge scissors, cut note card into 4" x 5" rectangle and mount to lid with spray mount adhesive. Use rubber stamps to make title for box on note card.

Step 9: Attach fabric daisies to centers of ribbon stripes with craft glue. Allow to dry overnight.

Small Box

MATERIALS
- Craft glue
- Double-stick tape
- Fabric flower: 1
- Kraft box: cream or vanilla, 4 1/2" round
- Needle and thread
- Ribbon: 1 1/2" yellow silk; 15" plaid French wired, 1 yard
- Velvet leaves: 12
- Vintage pearl buttons: 12

INSTRUCTIONS
Step 1: Attach 1" pieces of double-stick tape at 1" intervals to one side of yellow ribbon. Beginning at back of box, wrap around bottom of box, pressing firmly.

Step 2: Attach velvet leaves to edge of box lid with craft glue, overlapping just slightly.

Step 3: Attach button at each space in between leaves with craft glue.

Step 4: To create plaid flower base, hold length of ribbon in one hand, gather up to 4" at a time with other hand, and fold back over onto itself, meeting in middle every time and securing with your thumb. Rotate developing petals until you have created circle of six. Sew this bunch together by pulling knotted thread up from underneath center of circle. Secure with half a dozen stitches. Glue plaid flower base to center of lid with craft glue.

Step 5: Attach fabric flower to center of plaid ribbon base with craft glue. Allow to dry overnight.

Fairy Bottles

By Elaine Seamans
Page 34

Fallen Stars Bottle

MATERIALS

- Cotton balls
- Glass bottle
- Glass stars: enough to fill bottle 1/3 full
- Paper
- Paraffin wax
- Pen
- Ribbon: for neck and bottom of bottle
- Shoe polish: brown
- Strong-hold glue or hot glue gun
- Wire: thin brass or silver

TOOLS

- Double boiler (for melting wax)
- Scissors

INSTRUCTIONS

Step 1: Using thin wire, wrap two or three stars together individually, crisscrossing wire across star about two times. Leave long piece of wire (relative to length of bottle and how far you want star to hang from top). Bend wire so it is coming off top point of star and it hangs straight. Do this to each star you plan to hang.

Step 2: Hang stars from top of bottle at varying lengths so they are not touching each other. Secure wire to top of bottle; glue to edge. Secure stars to bottle with glue.

Step 3: "Cork" bottle with cotton ball. Dip "corked" end of bottle in melted paraffin wax that has been melted in double boiler and is still liquid. Dip many times to create cloudy, opaque effect. The hotter the wax, the clearer and thinner it will be. The colder the wax, the more opaque and thick it will be.

Step 4: Write "Fallen Stars" on paper and hand tear edges. To create aged look, rub edges with cotton ball smeared with brown shoe polish. Coat back of paper with thin film of glue and place on bottle.

Step 5: Glue decorative ribbon to bottom and neck of bottle.

Fallen Fairy Wings Bottle

MATERIALS

- Cotton balls
- Glass beads (to string on ribbon)
- Glass bottle
- Glitter: opalescent
- Paper
- Pen
- Ribbon: very thin, silk
- Ribbon or trim (to decorate neck of bottle)
- Shoe polish: brown
- Strong-hold glue
- Velvet leaves: 2, in colors associated with fairies

TOOLS

■ Double boiler
  (for melting wax)

■ Scissors

INSTRUCTIONS

Step 1: Twist wire stems of leaves and combine with thin silk ribbon. String beads on ribbon.

Step 2: Tie ribbon in half knot (look should be loose). Cut ribbon to length that flows down middle of leaf "wings," with some to spare for draping. Place leaves in bottle with sides going in first (not wires). Toss in some pinches of glitter.

Repeat steps 3-5 of Fallen Stars Bottle.

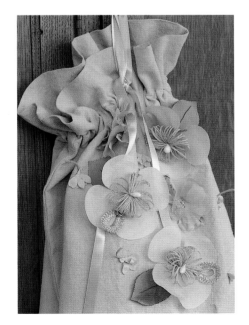

Laundry Bag

By Kaari Meng
Page 35

MATERIALS

■ Cord or ribbon: 1 yard
  (for pull)

■ Fabric: cream linen, 1 ½ yard

■ Millinery leaves, flowers, and stamens

■ Safety pin

TOOLS

■ Hot glue gun or fabric glue

■ Scissors

■ Sewing machine

INSTRUCTIONS

Step 1: Cut fabric and sew bag to desired shape. Basic laundry bag is 35" length x 24" width. Leave top open and sew 1" open envelope 3" down from top of bag.

Step 2: Thread cord or ribbon through this envelope by attaching one end to safety pin and pulling through. Once pulled through, tie into loose bow.

Step 3: Arrange millinery flowers, leaves, and stamens on bag. Placing a board between the two layers, glue embellishments in place with hot glue gun or fabric glue. Hang bag on doorknob or at end of bedpost to brighten up room and inspire you to do laundry!

Blooming Bed Linens and Duvet

By Richie Rich and Traver Rains
Pages 40-45

MATERIALS

■ Appliqués (to mix with faux flowers and leaves)

■ Bed linens: bed sheets—cotton, 1 bottom sheet, 1 top sheet; duvet cover—cotton, 1; pillowcases—cotton, 2 king-size

■ Fabric dye: colors of your choice

■ Fabric silk-screen paint

■ Faux flowers and leaves: as many as desired

■ Needle and thread

■ Pompom fringe: enough to trim top edges of top sheet and edges of pillowcases

■ Poster board

■ Salt

- Silk fringe: enough to trim top of duvet cover
- Sponge
- Tassels: coordinating colors, 8

Optional: Glitter, sequins, and buttons

TOOLS
- Iron
- Scissors
- Sewing machine

INSTRUCTIONS

Step 1: Fill large tub with fabric dye, hot water, and salt (to maintain color). Mix dye according to package instructions. Stir well; colors can be mixed to achieve hues you desire. Repeat process for each color you wish to use. Rinse well with cold water. For tie-dye effect, dip edges of items into different colors.

Step 2: Dry and iron all pieces.

Step 3: Using poster board, cut out shapes (hearts, stars, moons, etc.). With sponge and silk-screen paint, blot designs onto fabric.

Step 4: Sew trim around edges (pompoms, fringe, etc.).

Step 5: Hand sew flowers onto corners of pillowcases, duvet, and wherever else desired. Glitter, sequins, and buttons also can be added.

Step 6: Add tassels to corners of pillowcases.

Dry cleaning recommended.

Fluffed-Up Slippers

By Marcia Ceppos

Page 43

MATERIALS
- Appliqués: felt flowers, 2 large and 2 small
- Felt balls: 8 in assorted colors
- Pompom fringe: 12" or enough to cover top edge of slippers
- Ribbon and trim: 24" each in contrasting colors
- Slippers: slip-on

TOOLS
- Hot glue gun or fabric glue
- Measuring tape
- Scissors

INSTRUCTIONS

Step 1: Measure length of top edge of slipper for pompom fringe and cut. Measure length of top of inner sole and measure one length of ribbon; trim for each slipper.

Step 2: Glue narrow ribbon along top edge of inner sole. Glue contrasting trim inside ribbon.

Step 3: Glue pompom fringe along top inside curve of slipper, meeting at narrow ribbon on sides.

Step 4: Arrange appliqués, flowers, and felt balls in any pattern you prefer and glue to top of slipper. Add one yellow felt ball at back of slipper, just for fun.

Laundry Hamper

By Marcia Ceppos
Page 47

MATERIALS
- Faux flowers: your choice
- Hamper basket
- Tassels

TOOLS
- Hot glue gun or fabric glue

INSTRUCTIONS
Note: You may choose to spray paint basket to fit with your room décor.

Step 1: Arrange flowers on all four top and bottom corners of hamper as desired and glue in place.

Step 2: Knot tassels to lid and handles.

Musical Memo Board

By Anna Corba
Page 51

MATERIALS
- Buttons: vintage, 2
- Cardboard: 1/4" corrugated, 18" x 14"
- Charms (to cover tops of thumbtacks)
- Clean cloth
- Decoupage medium
- Double-stick tape
- Ribbon: 2 1/2" lime silk, 1 yard; 1 1/2" purple silk, 1 yard; desired width for hanging, bright orange grosgrain, 1 yard
- Sheet music
- Tacky glue
- Thumbtacks
- Vintage green daisy, 1
- Vintage postcard
- Vintage velvet leaf, 1

TOOLS
- Scissors

INSTRUCTIONS
Step 1: Using decoupage medium, cover cardboard with sheet music. Wrap around back and miter edges for clean look. Press out air bubbles with clean cloth.

Step 2: Attach 1" pieces of double-stick tape to one side of purple and lime green ribbons at 2" intervals. Stick center of lime green ribbon at base of board and wrap around sides, adhering at board's back.

Step 3: Overlap purple ribbon same way, being certain edges lie straight, creating even stripe.

Step 4: Snip pointed tails at one end of pink ribbon. Fold ribbon and attach to center of lime and purple ribbon in middle of board.

Step 5: Attach velvet leaf over pink ribbon with glue. Attach daisy above leaf with glue.

Step 6: Attach orange grosgrain ribbon to back of board with thumbtacks, 1" from top outer edge of board.

Step 7: Glue charms to heads of thumbtacks to create decorative pins for holding items to board.

Step 8: Enlarge vintage post-card and use as focal point on board, allowing other items to gather around it.

Ribbon Clutch

By Lorren Bell
Page 53

MATERIALS

- Fabric clutch or handbag
- Ribbons and trims: enough to cover clutch
- Silk flower: 1

TOOLS

- Hot glue gun
- Measuring tape
- Scissors

INSTRUCTIONS

Note: Choose fabric clutch or handbag with clean lines at thrift store or discount outlet.

Step 1: Measure width of bag and cut ribbon and trim strips accordingly. Apply glue to edges of first pieces of ribbon and place along top edge of bag.

Step 2: Repeat with additional strips of ribbon, placing them edge-to-edge until you reach bottom of bag.

Step 3: Apply strips of decorative trim across inside edges of ribbon and then around perimeter of bag. Start under where flower will be placed to conceal seam.

Step 4: Glue flower in place.

Jewel of Light

By Gerard Yosca
Page 55

MATERIALS

- Appliqués: assorted
- Brass buttons: assorted
- Eye pins: brass
- Head pins: brass
- Ribbon: assorted, 10 yards
- Rickrack trim
- Round beads
- Tear-shaped glass drops
- Tear-shaped pearl drops
- Tinsel trim: 1 yard
- Wire: 20 and 28 gauge

TOOLS

- Hot glue gun
- Long-handled wooden spoon
- Needle-nose pliers

- Scissors
- Wire cutter

INSTRUCTIONS

Note: Your color scheme may be very different than mine. Take time to study your fixture and scheme. You may want to take a digital photo of the fixture and experiment with color placement on a copy of the photo before you start.

Step 1: Disassemble fixture, using digital camera to document the process so you'll know exactly how it should go back together.

Step 2: Do a trial wrap with scrap ribbon around each part of the fixture. This will help to determine exact length of ribbon needed for wrapping each part. Be sure to use ribbon that's not so bulky that light will not fit back together.

Step 3: Wrap all parts of fixture with final ribbon you have chosen. Hot glue to secure end of each ribbon near edge of fixture piece. Reassemble fixture.

Step 4: Choose and affix trim to wrapped parts of fixture. Add buttons, mirrors, jewelry, appliqués, rickrack, braid, and tinsel. Wherever there is a joint you can add a row of tinsel trim.

Step 5: Add beads, buttons, and appliqués to arms of light fixture. Remember to be bold—this piece is likely to be viewed from a distance.

Step 6: Wrap 20-gauge brass wire tightly around handle of wooden spoon to make large coiled "spring." Remove coil and stretch out.

Step 7: Fit coil on arm of fixture. Clip off excess coil. Tie spiral to fixture in six places using 28-gauge wire.

Step 8: Using head pins and eye pins, make drops by stringing beads over pin area. Attach drops to spiral.

Trimmed Linens

By Guillermo Guerra
Page 59

MATERIALS
- Pre-made pillowcase or sham
- Ribbon: enough to vertically wrap around pillowcase

TOOLS
- Hot glue gun or sewing machine
- Iron
- Scissors

INSTRUCTIONS

Step 1: Measure pillowcase around vertical center and cut ribbon accordingly.

Step 2: Sew or glue ribbon to center of pillowcase.

Note: It is recommended that pillowcase be washed and ironed prior to embellishing.

Leaf Wreath Picture

By Melissa Neufeld
Page 66

MATERIALS
- Chipboard or museum board

- Craft glue
- Fabric: vintage preferred, size of wreath
- Fabric leaves
- Paper: decorative, for background
- Picture frame with glass
- Postcard or other image for center of wreath
- Ribbon

TOOLS
- Scissors

INSTRUCTIONS
Step 1: Cover chipboard or museum board with decorative paper. Old sheet music was used for this project.

Step 2: Place and glue postcard in center of board.

Step 3: Glue leaves onto backside of fabric. Cut out leaves.

Step 4: Arrange fabric-covered leaves around picture or postcard to form wreath. Glue leaves down with craft glue. Set aside to dry completely.

Step 5: Tie ribbon into bow. Glue to wreath. Allow to dry.

Step 6: Insert board into picture frame.

Hand-Decorated Books

By Nancy Rosin
Page 67

MATERIALS
- Acrylic spray
- Books: sizes of choice
- Craft glue
- Embellishments: stars, tassels, etc., as desired
- Paper: enough to cover front and back of books
- Paper towel or tissue
- Ribbon: 3", enough to cover circumference of books and

length of spine plus 2" for overlap on top and bottom; any additional ribbon, as desired
- Rubber cement

TOOLS
- Hot glue gun
- Scissors

INSTRUCTIONS
Step 1: Place book on paper and cut paper slightly larger than book.

Step 2: Generously apply rubber cement to underside of paper and apply to book. Use paper towel or tissue to gently burnish paper to book. Press out excess glue past edges of book and remove. Allow to dry.

Step 3: Using sharp scissors, cut along edges of book to remove extra paper.

Step 4: Position 3"-wide ribbon along spine of book. Fold over at least 1" of width of ribbon to front and 1" to back of book. Adhere ribbon with craft glue. You have created a ribbon spine.

Step 5: Adhere other ribbons to front and back of book covers as desired.

Step 6: Bring 1" of edges of ribbons over upper and lower edges and glue on inner side of book. If you prefer to add ribbon at corners, follow same procedure.

Step 7: Apply other embellishments as desired.

Dupioni Pillowcases

By Guillermo Guerra

Page 72

MATERIALS
- Fabric: dupioni silk, approximately 1 1/2 yards per pillowcase
- Pillowcase (to use as pattern)
- Ribbon or trim: long enough to go around vertical height of pillowcase

TOOLS
- Iron
- Scissors
- Sewing machine

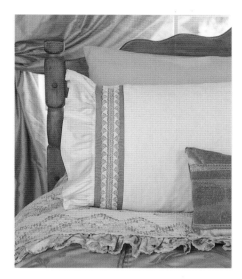

INSTRUCTIONS

Step 1: Using pre-made pillowcase as pattern, fold fabric in half; place pillowcase on top and cut around already-made case. Save remainder of fabric to use as ruffled edge, if desired.

Step 2: With right sides together, sew pillowcase on three sides, leaving one narrow side open. Finish fourth side with hemstitch or ruffle. Turn right side out and press.

Step 3: Sew ribbon or trim about 1/2" from open end of pillowcase.

Pillow Sachets

By Rosemary Warren

Page 77

MATERIALS
- Dried lavender
- Fabric: vintage or silk, 1/4 yard
- Needle and thread
- Ribbon: to coordinate with fabric, 1 1/3 yard

TOOLS
- Iron
- Scissors
- Sewing machine

INSTRUCTIONS

Step 1: Cut two pieces of fabric into 8" squares.

Step 2: Place right sides together and sew three sides with machine.

Step 3: Turn inside out and press.

Step 4: Fill with lavender and sew fourth side closed by hand with needle and thread.

Step 5: Tie sachet with ribbon as you would tie gift box.

Lavender-Filled Pillow

By Kaari Meng

Page 85

MATERIALS

- Dried lavender
- Fabric: decorative, such as brocade, to cover front of pillow; thin cotton to hold lavender
- Needle and thread
- Pillow
- Trim: enough to run around all four edges of decorative fabric

TOOLS

- Hot glue gun
- Scissors
- Sewing machine

INSTRUCTIONS

Note: This project can be made with any size pillow. In this project a king-size pillow was used.

Step 1: Cut two pieces of fabric size needed to make envelope slightly shorter than height of pillow and same width as pillow.

Step 2: With right sides together, sew three sides of fabric together with sewing machine.

Step 3: Fill fabric envelope with dried lavender. Sew fourth side of envelope closed by hand.

Step 4: Attach fabric envelope to pillow using hot glue gun around all four edges of envelope.

Step 5: Finish edges of envelope with trim, using hot glue gun to attach it.

Ribbon Bolster

By Linda Ashton

Page 85

MATERIALS

- Pillow: standard size, down-filled
- Cord: 31" lengths, 2 (used to gather sides)
- Fabric: 27" x 27"
- Fabric glue
- Pin backs: 2
- Ribbon: 27" lengths of assorted ribbon of your choice
- Rosettes: 2
- Straight pins
- Thread (to match each ribbon color)

TOOLS

- Iron
- Scissors
- Sewing machine

INSTRUCTIONS

Step 1: Iron fabric and then lay flat on table.

Step 2: Arrange ribbons from top to bottom in straight lines. Ribbons can be side by side or with enough space between to show fabric underneath. (Leave 2" at each side for ribbon gussets.)

Step 3: Pin in place to secure position. Machine sew at edges of ribbon smoothly, or glue down with fabric glue.

Step 4: To create side gussets: Fold down sides of fabric 1/2". Pin and iron down smoothly. Remove pins. Fold ironed fold again another 1/2" and pin and iron smoothly. Sew close to inside folded edge to create tube to feed cord through.

Step 5: Run cord through gusset created, extending 2" at each end. Knot each end of cord to keep it from slipping inside.

Step 6: To complete pillow: Fold fabric right sides together and join top and bottom edges. Make sure ribbons are lined up where they will meet. Pin edges together. *Note:* Be sure not to pin or

sew gussets with cord running through them. Sew 1" from edge, joining top and bottom without sewing gussets.

Step 7: Turn fabric right side out. Pull ribbon or cord on one side tightly until it will not pull anymore. Tie off with secure bow.

Step 8: Stuff down pillow inside and pull ribbon to close other side. A bolster shape will be formed.

Step 9: Attach pin backs to rosettes with glue and pin over side openings, or glue them on.

Bed Tray

By Jill Schwartz
Page 86

MATERIALS

- Acrylic paint
- Appliqués
- Buttons
- Doily
- Foam adhesive mounting tape
- Glass: cut to fit dimension of drawer
- Glitter
- Images or photographs (to use in collage on tray)
- Paintbrush
- Paper towel
- Ribbon: enough to inset into recesses of tray and strong and long enough for handles
- Shallow drawer
- Strong-hold glue or epoxy
- Vintage flowers: silk or velvet
- Wood strips: 1/4" thick, dimensions of tray
- Wrapping paper

TOOLS

- Drill and screws
- Hot glue gun
- Ruler or tape measure
- Saw
- Scissors

INSTRUCTIONS

Step 1: Paint drawer inside and out.

Step 2: Measure interior of drawer and use saw to cut two ¼" strips length of drawer, and two strips equal to width of drawer. Make sure strips fit snugly, then paint them same color as drawer. Set aside.

Step 3: Measure width outside recesses of drawer. Cut and fit ribbon for each side. Affix adhesive mounting tape to one side of each ribbon. Remove backing from tape and mount inside each recess.

Step 4: Adhere appliqués, buttons, and/or flowers as desired to outside of drawer with strong-hold glue. *Note:* We chose to apply glitter to cloth doily before it was affixed to tray.

Step 5: Line bottom of inside of drawer with wrapping paper or other decorative paper. Arrange ornaments (appliqués, buttons, doily, flowers, images, etc., making sure all are under height of ½") on bottom inside of drawer. Glue down each piece.

Step 6: Place adhesive mounting tape around bottom, side, and part of top of each ¼" strip. Place wood strips on bottom inside edges of drawer, pressing firmly in place. This will serve as ledge to hold glass.

Step 7: Place glass over strips, pressing firmly in place so glass adheres to exposed mounting tape.

Step 8: Make handles by cutting ribbon in pieces long enough to make loops to fit your hand through. Screw ribbons in place on short sides of drawer.

Note: Remember that this ribbon will get hard use, so it should be sturdy.

Step 9: Decorate tops of screws with buttons attached with hot glue gun.

Decoupage Lampshade

By Kaari Meng
Page 87

MATERIALS
- Acrylic paint
- Lampshade

- Notions: cabochons, buttons, feathers, trim
- Old garden book
- Scraps of paper, old labels, cut-outs
- Water-based sealer glue, acid free

TOOLS
- Hot glue gun
- Paintbrush
- Scissors

INSTRUCTIONS

Step 1: Decide which garden-themed design you like; make multiple copies on printer.

Step 2: Cut out shapes as close to image as possible.

Step 3: Using water-based sealer glue, adhere paper bits to lampshade; let dry completely.

Step 4: If shapes are black and white, paint designs with desired colors; let dry completely.

Step 5: Paint layer of sealer over entire lampshade; let dry completely.

Step 6: Attach notions, buttons, feathers, or trim with hot glue gun.

Vanity Trinket Box & Powder Puff Wand

By Carole Sidlow
Page 87

Powder Puff Wand

MATERIALS

■ Fabric glue

■ Powder puff: approximately 4"

■ Ribbon: enough to wrap stick and 1 yard of ¼" ribbon to tie bow and streamers around stick

■ Stick for wand

INSTRUCTIONS

Step 1: Wrap stick with ribbon and glue in place.

Step 2: Glue puff to wand.

Step 3: Make ribbon rose and leaves per following Ribbon Rose and Leaves instructions and affix to back of powder puff. Tie bow and streamers in place.

Trinket Box

MATERIALS

■ Box: kraft paper or wood, small

■ Fabric glue

■ Ribbon: width and length of top and bottom sides of box

INSTRUCTIONS

Step 1: Adhere ribbon around sides of box top and bottom with fabric glue.

Step 2: Make ribbon rose and leaves per following Ribbon Rose and Leaves instructions and affix to top of box.

Ribbon Rose and Leaves

MATERIALS

■ Fabric glue

■ Lace: 1 ¼" white or ecru border lace, 1 ½ yards

■ Ribbon: ½" satin ribbon, 1 ½ yards; 1 ½" green satin ribbon (for leaves), ⅓ yard; wired ombre ribbon (for cabbage rose), ½ yard

TOOLS

■ Scissors

■ Sewing machine

INSTRUCTIONS

Step 1: Gather border lace into circle to overlap top of trinket box and top of powder puff. Glue to top of each project.

Step 2: Rouche (Diagram 1) 1 ½ yards of ½" satin ribbon. Ribbon

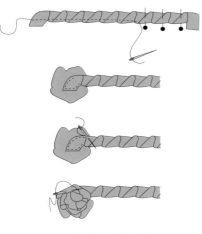

DIAGRAM 1

is rouched by sewing zigzag basting stitch and gathering it from one end.

Step 3: Attach rouched ribbon over lace border circle with fabric glue, leaving room for cabbage rose.

Step 4: Make cabbage rose from ¹/₂ yard of wired ombre ribbon (Diagram 2) by folding on diagonal and sewing each corner to bottom of flower. Glue to top of box.

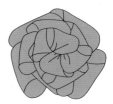

DIAGRAM 2

Step 5: Make ribbon leaves (Diagram 3) from ¹/₃ yard green satin ribbon. Tuck leaves between border lace circle and rouched ribbon and fix in place with fabric glue.

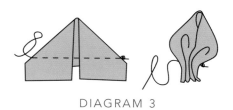

DIAGRAM 3

Parasol Lampshade

By Jill Schwartz
Page 95

MATERIALS
- Acrylic paint
- Fringe: enough to go around bottom circumference of parasol
- Parasol
- Stencil paper
- String
- Vintage-style flowers and leaves: assorted faux

TOOLS
- Craft knife
- Foam brush
- Hot glue gun
- Paintbrush
- Scissors

INSTRUCTIONS
Step 1: Open parasol and set in stable location. (A clean garbage can works well.)

Step 2: Cut dot pattern out of stencil paper with craft knife.

Step 3: Gently, but firmly, place stencil paper over lampshade. Dab paint over stencil paper with

foam brush and very little paint to create dot pattern on shade. Too much paint will bleed.

Step 4: Remove stencil paper and allow paint to dry.

Step 5: Measure bottom circumference of shade with string. Cut fringe to length of string, allowing small amount for overlap.

Step 6: Affix fringe to bottom of shade with hot glue gun.

Step 7: Arrange flowers and leaves as desired and affix to lampshade with hot glue gun.

Bulletin Dress Form

By Rosemary Warren
Page 95

MATERIALS
- Antique buttons
- Clear pushpins

- ■ Craft glue: quick-dry
- ■ Dress form
- ■ Lace or netting
- ■ Straight pins
- ■ Stretch velvet ribbon: 4 yards

TOOLS
- ■ Scissors

INSTRUCTIONS

Step 1: Cover body of dress form with lace or netting, stretching it over front and pinning it in back. Cut off excess; glue in place, if desired.

Step 2: Crisscross stretch ribbon four times around form and secure in place in back with pins.

Step 3: Cover tops of clear pushpins with buttons using quick-dry craft glue. Insert pushpins at front of form where ribbons meet.

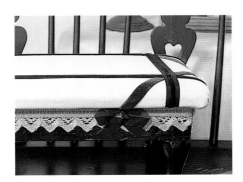

Tudor Footstool

By Melissa Neufeld
Page 97

MATERIALS

- ■ Fabric: enough to recover stool
- ■ Lace: metallic, enough to cover circumference of stool
- ■ Ribbon: velvet, enough to run down length and width of stool twice plus enough to make four bows (for this project, black velvet striped and red stretch velvet were used)
- ■ Trim: gold, enough to go around all sides of stool
- ■ Upholstered stool
- ■ Upholstery tacks: decorative, if available

TOOLS

- ■ Hot glue gun
- ■ Scissors

- ■ Screwdriver
- ■ Staple gun
- ■ Staple remover (if necessary to remove old fabric)

INSTRUCTIONS

Step 1: Remove upholstered seat from stool, using screwdriver if necessary. Use staple remover if fabric has been stapled to seat.

Step 2: Using old fabric as pattern, cut new fabric, allowing enough fabric to wrap over edges to bottom of seat.

Step 3: Attach new fabric to seat with staple gun. Be sure to pull tightly so there are no wrinkles.

Step 4: Arrange ribbon in desired pattern on seat of stool and affix at undersides with staple gun.

Step 5: Tie four small bows and attach at ends of corner ribbons using decorative upholstery tacks.

Step 6: Attach lace and trim to circumference of stool, just under seat, using hot glue gun.

Step 7: Reattach seat to stool with screwdriver and screws.

The Designers

LINDA ASHTON

Linda is a milliner with more than 10 years experience designing hats with a whimsical spirit. A graduate of the Fashion Institute of Technology's millinery program, Linda has created hats for celebrities, designers, and many discerning customers. Her inspired custom designs are influenced by original fabrications, textures, and colors with impeccable attention to detail.

Linda divides her time between her two homes, a New York apartment and a narrowboat in London's Little Venice. **www.lindaashton.com**

LORREN BELL

A native of Canton, Ohio, Lorren set off for New York at age 22, armed with a passion for fashion and a sensible business degree. He launched his accessories company, Deluxe by Lorren Bell, in 1993 with the goal of marrying stylish form to practical function and weaving in indulgent whimsy. He quickly developed a devoted following, when buyers across the country embraced his innovative use of Swarovski crystal and faux tortoise. He expanded his high-end glamour-infused costume jewelry business to include luxury hair ornaments and hip home accents, and in 1996, he launched a chic embellished handbag collection. The brand is sold in department stores and boutiques on three continents. Lorren expanded into retail in 1999, opening his first store in Dallas, Texas.

Lorren's work has appeared in countless fashion publications and he is a regular source for costume designers, working on projects ranging from "Miss Congeniality" to "The Cybil Show." He has been privileged to design many items for DIFFA, and in 2003, Lorren joined the board of directors of Fashion Group International.

MARCIA CEPPOS

Growing up in Queens, New York, I toted around a tennis racquet, baseball bat, or any other athletic implement, but certainly not an artist's palette. During my college days, you could always find me on the tennis court. While I always knew I would work at Tinsel Trading, it never occurred to me that it would be in a designer capacity. I just liked being around all of the "stuff."

As I began spending more time at Tinsel Trading, my new second home, I talked to designers in all fields, including interiors, clothing, jewelry, and millinery, trying to learn as much as possible. Perhaps by osmosis, or just a hidden talent awakened, I began designing new trims. Once I saw the wonderful result of these initial attempts, there was no stopping me.

I have been very, very fortunate to have the materials, the venue, and most important, the audience, to allow me to see my efforts realized and appreciated. There are still times I miss the adrenaline rush from hitting the perfect passing shot down the line…however, the thrill I get from designing trims is almost as spectacular. **www.tinseltrading.com**

ANNA CORBA

Anna's journey in collage art began when her collections refused to lay tame on her studio shelves. Paper ephemera, found objects, and ribbon began making their way into her paintings, and as a way of sustaining her newfound calling she created a product line that uses these materials in a functional yet whimsical manner.

Anna's journals, tags, candles, and cake pedestals can be found in specialty stores across the country. She is the author of *Vintage Paper Crafts* (Sterling/Chapelle ©2004) and *Making Memory Boxes* (Sterling/Chapelle ©2005). Anna lives with her sculptor husband in Northern California and works out of her carriage house studio with her dog, Caylus, at her feet. **e-mail:** foundcatstudio@msn.com

GUILLERMO GUERRA

Guillermo Guerra is an accomplished fashion and interior designer. While in Austin, Texas, he established a successful design firm. There he worked on both residential and commercial projects that included local restaurants Jeffrey's and Shoreline Grill. Guillermo, now living in New York City, has launched a successful line of unique T-shirts available on the East Coast and West Coast.

LESLIE KORDA

Leslie has been making and decorating things for as long as she can remember. To satisfy her mother's insistence that she have something to fall back on, she bought a comfortable couch and then graduated from Pratt Institute with a degree in Industrial Design. Since then she has worked in graphic design, kitchen and bath design, and for the past 15 years, jewelry design. Leslie refers to her original style as elegant-funky, combining disparate materials with an occasionally off-beat idea.

KAARI MENG

Kaari Meng began her first business—a line of vintage glass jewelry—on West 38th Street in New York City back in 1992, across the street from Tinsel Trading. She has since moved to the West Coast and opened French General, a vintage textile and notion shop, in Hollywood, California. Inspired by color and texture, French General was developed as a decorating shop for the home. As well as custom textile work, French General also creates vintage craft kits for people intrigued with notions, millinery, and ephemera. Long an admirer of Marcia Ceppos and her treasure trove, Kaari was honored to contribute to this book. **www.frenchgeneral.com**

MELISSA NEUFELD

During the 10 years she was president of Melissa Neufeld, Inc., Melissa manufactured and sold gift wrap, tissue paper, stickers, magnets, stationery, soaps, and other bath products. She held the original license for the manufacture and sale of Mary Engelbreit's stickers, magnets, and playing cards.

Melissa has worked with Martha Stewart on cooking seminars at Sterling Vineyards in California and on her Christmas book. She has appeared many times on Martha's television show, demonstrating how to make gift and designer items. She is currently designing for Barbara Schriber Designs and resides in Danville, California.

RICHIE RICH AND TRAVER RAINS

Richie Rich trained with Kristi Yamaguchi to be a competitive skater and was ranked 12th in the nation. He used his theatrical talent and what he learned watching seamstresses backstage at the Ice Capades and began making clothes for his performances.

Like Richie, Traver needed great-looking clothing at affordable prices so he began designing and sewing his own vests and chaps. After attending college in Texas, Traver received a degree in Economics and International Business and then moved to New York to pursue other endeavors.

Richie and Traver are the designers behind Heatherette, a custom ready-to-wear clothing line known for its outrageous style that began in December 1999. When Richie showed up at a party in one of his own leather tops, a buyer for the store Patricia Field ordered 20 of the tops on the spot. After seeing the line at Patricia Field, hip-hop star Foxy Brown asked Richie and Traver to design her outfits for the MTV Video Music Awards. Word spread and soon Mariah Carey and Gwen Stefani were fans. **www.heatherette.com**

NANCY ROSIN

Inspired by the art and history of antique valentines, and fascinated by the entire realm of ephemera, Nancy Rosin has made valentines her creative focus. Her presence on television—notably "Martha Stewart Living" and "The Incurable Collector"—has made her indelibly linked with her romantic subject. Her annual "Live Valentine Chat" is the longest-running event of its kind on eBay.

Nancy creates custom greeting cards, designs for boxes, valentine kits, and scrapbooking books.

Nancy's valentines have been featured in a video, "The Valentine and Expressions of Love," and she has authored numerous books including *Memories of a Lifetime: Vintage Labels—Perfume and Linens* and *Memories of a Lifetime: Fairies & Angels—Artwork for Scrapbooks & Fabric-Transfer Crafts* published by Sterling/Chapelle.
www.victoriantreasury.com

MICHAEL SCHULTZ

Designer and principal of Motel Deluxe Inc., Michael Schultz is a high-end wholesaler of gift and stationery items based in New York City.

This project was a homecoming of sorts for Michael. A decade ago, while his company was in its infancy, Michael was approached to design curtain panels for ABC Carpet & Home, the venerable Manhattan retailer. "When the business began, we were selling everything from handmade greeting cards to lighting," says Michael. "The common thread was the use of sheer fabrics and vintage trims. ABC Carpet had been one of our first customers and their buyer approached me at a trade show and asked if I could design curtains and pillows to go with the lighting they were already buying. Of course I said yes, even though I had never made either before."

Michael continues to use vintage trims in new and innovative ways and cites Tinsel Trading as a constant source of inspiration.

JILL SCHWARTZ

Jill, the daughter of a graphic artist and an interior designer, was raised with an appreciation of art, which was one of the cornerstones of her upbringing. Jill was fascinated with jewelry at an early age, and at 3, she glued beads to her ear lobes.

The jewelry, frames, journals, and books Jill designs are a natural synthesis of her training similar to that of her parents—graphic art and interior design. They incorporate her love and knowledge of ancient and ethnic arts, and are distinguished by a wonderfully balanced collage and assemblage.

Stores and catalogs such as Anthropologie, J. Jill, Barneys, and Neiman Marcus are among the many retailers that carry Jill's designs produced by her company, "Elements."

ELAINE SEAMANS

Elaine's inspiration is found in fairy tales, Shakespeare, nature, textures, wise people, and wise dogs. One of her major inspirations has been from her dachshund, Quackers, who passed away in 1998.

Her company, At-Choo, was created many moons ago and has evolved from designing ornate brooches to baby christening gowns and journals, stationery, pet items, wacky fairy bottles, and sterling silver and gold jewelry.

Elaine was honored by Victoria magazine as one of 40 women entrepreneurs in the United States. The following year, she received the same recognition from Working Woman Magazine.

At-Choo designs are carried in high-end boutiques throughout the United States, Canada, England, and Germany. **www.at-choo.com**

CAROLE SIDLOW

Carole opened her first store in Los Angeles, California in 1979, specializing in antique laces, linens, quilts, and Victorian whimsies. She realized that there was a need for good ribbon that could not be found in craft and hobby stores. She set out to find beautiful ribbon for special projects.

In the last decade, Carole has discovered gorgeous ribbons from around the world, including those made in Europe by factories turning out lovely reproductions. In 1994, she moved to Nevada, where she operates a mail-order business. She specializes in exquisite ribbon, including vintage and antique. She supplies her line to doll costumers, milliners, quilters, and specialty collectors. **www.ribbonstore.com**

ROSEMARY WARREN

Rosemary is the creative mind behind the redesign of Tinsel Trading and its sister stores, The Store Next Door and The Store Across the Street. She has been working with Marcia Ceppos for more than a decade. She is the buyer, merchandiser manager, and visualist for all locations.

Prior to coming to New York, Rosemary designed floral and millinery creations from her Studio Rabbitworks Flora for 15 years in West Hollywood, California. Her work has been featured in Vogue, New York Magazine, Elle, and Glamour. Her clients include Rosanna Arquette, Julia Louis-Dreyfuss, Sela Ward, Steve Tisch, and James and Lois Garner.

Rosemary works between California, New York, and Atlanta, where she freelances and works trade shows for Tinsel Trading. **e-mail:** Rosemary@tinseltrading.com

GERARD YOSCA

One of the United States' most established fashion jewelry designers and a member on the Board of Directors of the Council of Fashion Designers of America, Gerard has developed a singular style over the past 25 years. This style combines his knowledge of past and current trends, a keen sense of color, a sense of humor, and personal vision.

His themes and materials constantly change, yet fine craftsmanship is his mantra. He works with Swarovski crystals, vintage glass stones, semi-precious minerals, fresh-water pearls, carved woods, and hand-spun glass pearls dipped in 14 coats of lacquer.

A native New Yorker, Gerard is a regular at the Sunday flea markets, always in search of his next source of inspiration, whether it's a glazed pot with cast iron detail or a pattern from a floral coverlet. His jewelry is showcased in department and specialty stores throughout the United States, Europe, and Asia including Saks Fifth Avenue, Bergdorf Goodman, Neiman Marcus, and Fenwick's of London.

PHOTOGRAPHER
ART GRAY

Architectural photographer Art Gray is the creative genius who shot every photo in this book. He is published in every major design magazine in the world, including Architectural Digest and Architectural Record Interior Design. His work also is featured in many architecture and interior design books, including *Brave New Houses* and *Hollywood Style*.

Art studied architecture at University of Michigan and photography at Brooks Institute in Santa Barbara, California. He has become a leading force in documenting the work of emerging architects and interior designers from Los Angeles. Art lives at the beach in Venice, California.

www.artgrayphotography.com

Acknowledgments

APPLAUSE AND OVATIONS

Have you ever noticed how many people, when winning awards, thank everyone they have ever met?

Sounds hokey, but I agree with them. To reach this point in my professional life was a lot of hard work, some luck, and a culmination of many past and present experiences and relationships.

There have been tons and tons of people who have helped me get to this point, but I will keep it brief and only name a few.

APPLAUSE

From what seems like another lifetime ago—Gracie, Lizzie, Ingrid, Wendy, Elizabeth, Debora, and Laura.

To my family, who thought I might be in need of a real job when I graduated college but were willing to hang in there with me anyway.

To my current staff for minding the store, literally, and for their support. Extra applause for Leslie, Will, and Massiel. Whistling along with applause for Anna and Linda, who kept the place going while I was hunched over the keyboard, trying to come up with pearls of wisdom, insights, and inspiration.

To Eileen, for giving me the opportunity to do this book and for her trust and confidence in my ability.

SPECIAL APPLAUSE

To Becky Vizard for entrusting us with her remarkable antique textile pillows. More incredible pillows are available on her website www.bviz.com.

To Rosemary Warren for loaning her vintage hat collection for our bedrooms.

To Jill Schwartz for allowing us to use her wonderful picture frames that are sprinkled throughout the book.

To Trisha Chasse for creating the amazing floral arrangement in The Autumn Bedroom with flowers from The Store Next Door and insects from Tinsel Trading.

To all the bedroom owners, who allowed us to reveal their intimate spaces.

STANDING OVATIONS

To all of the artists who took time out from their own busy schedules to contribute something special for this book. I hope they had fun and this leads to other adventures and incredible designs.

A special ovation to Melissa Neufeld and Kaari Meng, for their generosity and their constant flow of ideas for projects.

To Will, who changed hats and became an invaluable assistant to both Rosemary and Art.

RESOUNDING OVATION

To Art Gray, thank you for saying yes. I "shutter" at the thought if you had not agreed. You have an innate talent for capturing the story. Every shot of yours I have ever seen is beautiful with so much attention to detail. Your commitment to this book from inception and the experience you brought with you was more than I could have hoped. I am honored by your enthusiasm and the respect you show for Tinsel. Watching you and Roe lay out the storyboard on the floor is a sight I will always remember. Thank you for your loyalty and the years of friendship. We have both come a long way since we walked down Main Street in Santa Monica, laughing at the yuppies using cell phones.

A THUNDEROUS OVATION

To Roe, I have known you for more than 14 years and am still constantly amazed by your talent and vision. I could not have done this book without you, no really! The answer to Eileen would have been "thank you, but no." Your involvement in Tinsel Trading has brought it soaring to heights I could never have dreamed of. Your excitement, respect, and love for all Tinsel is as great as mine. Your imaginative and spectacular window displays for all of the stores, the creative merchandising ideas, and the task of head buyer for The Store Next Door (and the seemingly easy job of forecasting popular colors) have all contributed to the success. Who would have thought that hot summer day in July 1992, when you casually mentioned how you would love to do a window for Tinsel, would have been the start of an amazing relationship? I hope we continue to collaborate for a very long time. *Scusi, sono americana e parlo poco l'italiano. Mille grazie migliore amica.*

LAST BUT CERTAINLY NOT LEAST… A PERPETUAL OVATION

To my grandfather, Arch J. Bergoffen. His love of all things metal led him through a lifelong adventure that he chose to share with me. I thank him and hope to be as fortunate.

Credits

A RED LIPS 4 COURAGE BOOK

Eileen Cannon Paulin, Jayne Cosh,
Rebecca Ittner, Catherine Risling
8502 East Chapman Avenue, 303
Orange, CA 92869

www.redlips4courage.com

BOOK EDITOR

Eileen Cannon Paulin

COPY EDITOR

Catherine Risling

GRAPHIC DESIGN

Kehoe + Kehoe Design Associates
Burlington, VT

STYLIST

Rosemary Warren

PHOTOGRAPHY

Art Gray

METRIC EQUIVALENCY CHARTS

inches to millimeters and centimeters
mm-millimeters   cm-centimeters

inches	mm	cm	inches	cm	inches	cm
1/8	3	0.3	9	22.9	30	76.2
1/4	6	0.6	10	25.4	31	78.7
1/2	13	1.3	12	30.5	33	83.8
5/8	16	1.6	13	33.0	34	86.4
3/4	19	1.9	14	35.6	35	88.9
7/8	22	2.2	15	38.1	36	91.4
1	25	2.5	16	40.6	37	94.0
1 1/4	32	3.2	17	43.2	38	96.5
1 1/2	38	3.8	18	45.7	39	99.1
1 3/4	44	4.4	19	48.3	40	101.6
2	51	5.1	20	50.8	41	104.1
2 1/2	64	6.4	21	53.3	42	106.7
3	76	7.6	22	55.9	43	109.2
3 1/2	89	8.9	23	58.4	44	111.8
4	102	10.2	24	61.0	45	114.3
4 1/2	114	11.4	25	63.5	46	116.8
5	127	12.7	26	66.0	47	119.4
6	152	15.2	27	68.6	48	121.9
7	178	17.8	28	71.1	49	124.5
8	203	20.3	29	73.7	50	127.0

yards to meters

yards	meters	yards	meters	yards	meters	yards	meters	yards	meters
1/8	0.11	2 1/8	1.94	4 1/8	3.77	6 1/8	5.60	8 1/8	7.43
1/4	0.23	2 1/4	2.06	4 1/4	3.89	6 1/4	5.72	8 1/4	7.54
3/8	0.34	2 3/8	2.17	4 3/8	4.00	6 3/8	5.83	8 3/8	7.66
1/2	0.46	2 1/2	2.29	4 1/2	4.11	6 1/2	5.94	8 1/2	7.77
5/8	0.57	2 5/8	2.40	4 5/8	4.23	6 5/8	6.06	8 5/8	7.89
3/4	0.69	2 3/4	2.51	4 3/4	4.34	6 3/4	6.17	8 3/4	8.00
7/8	0.80	2 7/8	2.63	4 7/8	4.46	6 7/8	6.29	8 7/8	8.12
1	0.91	3	2.74	5	4.57	7	6.40	9	8.23
1 1/8	1.03	3 1/8	2.86	5 1/8	4.69	7 1/8	6.52	9 1/8	8.34
1 1/4	1.14	3 1/4	2.97	5 1/4	4.80	7 1/4	6.63	9 1/4	8.46
1 3/8	1.26	3 3/8	3.09	5 3/8	4.91	7 3/8	6.74	9 3/8	8.57
1 1/2	1.37	3 1/2	3.20	5 1/2	5.03	7 1/2	6.86	9 1/2	8.69
1 5/8	1.49	3 5/8	3.31	5 5/8	5.14	7 5/8	6.97	9 5/8	8.80
1 3/4	1.60	3 3/4	3.43	5 3/4	5.26	7 3/4	7.09	9 3/4	8.92
1 7/8	1.71	3 7/8	3.54	5 7/8	5.37	7 7/8	7.20	9 7/8	9.03
2	1.83	4	3.66	6	5.49	8	7.32	10	9.14

Index

WE LEAVE YOU
WITH THIS FINAL THOUGHT:

**Regardless of size, all beds and bedrooms
deserve to be embellished, embellished,
and embellished.**